Gay Marriage Considerations

A Review of *After the Ball*

Daniel V. Runyon, Ph.D.

Gay Marriage Considerations:
***A Review of* After the Ball**
Daniel V. Runyon, Ph.D.

Copyright 2015 by Daniel V. Runyon

The Voice™: Scripture taken from The Voice™. Copyright ©2006, 2007, 2008, 2012 by Ecclesia Bible Society.

Published by Saltbox Press, 167 Burr Oak Drive, Spring Arbor, Michigan 49283

ISBN: 978 1 878559 06 7

Price: $6.99

Contents

After the Ball contains seven chapters corresponding to the chapters below. In this book I summarize, paraphrase, and quote *Ball* and offer a few observations. Chapter eight is a concluding assessment of the current cultural trend and a recommendation for the true Church.

Introduction

In 2015 the Supreme Court of the United States of America and some lower courts considered making gay marriage legal throughout the nation. In just the past two decades homosexual behavior in America has gone from criminal offense to protected right. I consider this a paradigm shift worth considering.

I will consider gay marriage in the form of this book review looking back to 1989 when a watershed publication gave homosexuals in America the traction needed to bring about the gay revolution. I offer a few restrained observations in the course of this review, but mainly I let the self-evident worldview and values of this book speak for themselves.

Via interlibrary loan I received the musty book called *After the Ball: How America Will Conquer Its Fear and Hatred of Gays in the 90s,* by Marshall Kirk and Hunter Madsen (Doubleday, NY: 1989).

After the Ball was by Harvard graduate Marshall Kirk, a logician, poet, and researcher in neuropsychiatry. His co-author with a doctorate in politics from Harvard was Hunter Madsen who specialized in public persuasion tactics and social marketing. I will refer to the authors and their book collectively as *Ball* and use the gender neutral pronoun "it" whenever referencing the publication and its authors.

Published in 1989—about 20 years after I was in high school marching band and our flamboyantly gay drum major was one of the most popular kids in school and at the head of the class both socially and academically.

Ball begins by thanking those who helped write or inspire this "gay manifesto" and then provides the book outline revealed in my table of contents.

On page xvi of the introduction I discover that America is sick with "the wholehearted endorsement and practice of unvarnished *bigotry*" that "hates and eats its own" and "chews apart at least one homosexual child for every nine heterosexual children, and feeds it to them," resulting in high rates of suicide among gays. *Ball* begins to speak for God on page xvii when it asserts, "America rebukes all bigotry, except that which it imagines is God's." This line of reasoning will warrant careful attention.

I am left-handed, so the page xx allegory intrigues me: "Imagine what might have happened if society had come down with and pursued a grudge against the left-handed the way it has against gays," establishing that one in ten Americans is gay, just as one in ten Americans is left-handed. A page later, the allegory declares, "Raving and waving their scriptures, Judeo-Christian leaders encourage discrimination against lefties, because some Old Testament or other views left-handedness as the mark of Cain: 'For it is an abomination before God that a man shall do with his left hand what he would do with his right.'"

This allegory cautions me that I might do well to be aware of logical fallacies in *Ball*. "Faulty analogy comes to mind," as if left-handedness and homosexual acting out are morally equal. I realize that in spite of their Harvard degrees, these authors are either not well-versed in logic or assume their readers are easily deceived by deliberately flawed logic used as a manipulative technique. *Ball* may also be weak in moral sensibility, honestly thinking there is no God with a clearly defined moral template designed for the good of humanity.

The allegory presses forward, imagining forgiving and lenient churches that "permit left-handed to remain in their congregations so long as these unfortunates renounce vile, left-handed practices. Love the sinner, hate the sin!" (xxi). The allegory concludes that left-handedness doesn't matter: "Are not the love letters I write with my left hand still love letters? Are not the religious signs I make with my left hand still sincere gestures of my faith? Why am I persecuted for a handedness I came by naturally?" (xxii).

Note that every crime against humanity I could list is "come by naturally" and is part of the fallen condition of man. As I sit here, religious fanatics in Syria are slaughtering women and babies, following an instinct they came by naturally. We're still in the introduction, and *Ball* is already lost in a stew of logical fallacies.

I earned a Ph.D. studying the great 17th century allegories of English literature and sense that this left-handed allegory does not rise to the expected level, so I am relieved to hear *Ball* acknowledge its own "lefties" tale as ridiculous, yet it presses on to insist the weak allegory is an accurate portrayal of the gay situation. Providing no data beyond a few public opinion surveys, it plants in my mind an assumption that ten percent of the population is gay and acquired this sexual preference naturally.

I do not believe the 10% statistic for many reasons, the most objective one due to something called the "endogeneity" problems intrinsic in the so-called "research." Dr. Tim Groseclose, the Adam Smith Chair and Professor of Economics at George Mason University, told me in a personal interview on January 26, 2015, at Hillsdale College, that it takes about a year to guide a university student into a full understanding of endogeneity, so I certainly can't do it here.

To get an introduction to the endogeneity concept, I recommend pages 201-212 of his book *Left Turn: How Liberal Media Bias Distorts the American Mind* (St. Martins, 2011). Groseclose writes that "in science, some effects are *exogenous*, that is, outside the system, while others are endogenous, that is, inside the system. An endogeneity problem occurs when a researcher treats an effect as if it is exogenous, when it is actually *endogenous*" (Groseclose 204).

Entire books explore all the bias both inside and outside of research studies—the questions, the research subjects, the data analysis—and the skewed interpretation of such "research." Groseclose is a leading social-science researcher of our time and says such problems plague practically every study. Any interpretation of the data must be tentative and with a wide margin of error—which calls into question *Ball's* research data. Compared with Groseclose's exquisite scholarship, *Ball* reads like the musings of a child who never developed intellectually or emotionally beyond the "terrible twos." Psychological manipulation and name-calling are their foundational strategy.

A much larger problem for me is *Ball's* assumption that all "natural" human behaviors are wholesome and right and good and ought to be accepted and encouraged. Pay close attention to *Ball's* worldview. It made the hasty generalization of using the brand "bigot" on anyone who doesn't agree with it. Would these authors welcome similar branding of themselves? And if so, what are they really? Materialists? Hedonists? Narcissists?

I am beginning to suspect *Ball* has a very limited knowledge of human history. My own reading tastes are broad and eclectic. For example, another thing I read today is a sermon by Cyril, Bishop of Jerusalem in the fourth century, on the story of the paralytic by the pool in which he shows Jesus asking a man crippled 38 years, "Do you want to be healed?" Jesus heals the man, then later returns to warn the former paralytic, "See, you are cured. Do not sin anymore." Cyril then sternly gives his audience the same warning (see Edward Yarnold's translation of *Cyril of Jerusalem,* New York: Routledge, 2000).

No records indicate the onlookers lashed back at him, accusing him of harboring paralytic-phobia or paralytic-hate, but the tone of *Ball* so far indicates that is the response Cyril could anticipate if transported to this circumstance. *Ball* appears to want enabling, not healing.

Here's a point in *Ball* that gets to the root of its message: "'Homophobia' is a comforting word, isn't it? It suggests that our enemies...are actually scared of us!" So it knows this isn't true yet uses it as propaganda: "The very term 'phobia' ridicules our enemies (and intentionally so)" (xxiv).

I have wondered about this language for some time. I had gay friends in high school, a gay roommate in college, and have rubbed shoulders with quite a number of gay individuals. I never realized I was irrationally afraid of them—"phobia" is an irrational fear—and I now realize I have been intentionally branded with a deliberate lie. My hope of finding any hint of integrity in *Ball* is beginning to waiver. Propaganda consists of deliberate lies repeated often enough that they are assumed true. *Ball* was published 25 years ago, and in just that short time the propaganda it outlines has swayed a nation to believe something about itself that may be inaccurate.

Ball reports, "We've cast about in vain for a term that would, at once, (a) clearly signify 'homo-hatred' for the layman, (b) satisfy the pedant's demand for etymological consistency, and (c) for everyone, look as impressively scientistic and clinical as the term 'homophobia'" (xxv). So it coined the term 'homophobia' to tell me I am afraid of homosexuals and the term 'homohatred' to tell me, further, that I hate homosexuals. On the one hand I am insulted by their audacity at telling me things not true; on the other hand I am impressed by the success of their propaganda machine.

I wonder if reversing the etymology would be useful. Are these authors suffering from heterophobia; are they heterohaters? And if so, who will call them out on their potentially socially unacceptable attitudes?

The next section gloats about how AIDS has "brought us unprecedented public recognition and—along, of course, with a blast of increased hatred—gratifying sympathy" (xxvii). Then *Ball* gets to the crux of the matter: "The campaign we outline in this book, though complex, depends centrally upon a program of unabashed propaganda, firmly grounded in long-established principles of psychology and advertising" (xxviii).

In my left hand I read *Ball*; in my right hand I read a more carefully crafted and proven handbook for life, and today in that book I read, "There is nothing sacred, and no one is safe. Vicious sarcasm drips from their lips; they bully and threaten to crush their enemies. They even mock God as if He were not above; their arrogant tongues boast throughout the earth; they feel invincible. Even God's people turn and are carried away by them; they watch and listen, yet find no fault in them." (Psalm 73:8-10. All scripture quotes are from *The Voice*.)

Chapter 1

A Field Trip to Straight America

Ball is telling me that *homohatred* and *homophobia*—terms it appears to have just invented—function like the Great Wall of China to separate American society. They present "seven deadly myths" which I will summarize, but first it may be instructive to flesh out *Ball's* allusion to the seven deadly sins. Not having grown up Catholic, these categories don't come readily to my mind, but here they are:

1. **Lust** – to experience intense desire. Jesus said about this, "*You may think you have abided by this Commandment, walked the straight and narrow,* but I tell you that anyone who looks at a woman lustfully has already committed adultery with her in his heart" (Matthew 5:28).

2. **Gluttony** – to eat and drink to excess. Wisdom literature observes, "For both the drunk

and the glutton will end up broke, sleeping life away, and clothed in rags" (Proverbs 23:21).

3. Greed – the insatiable appetite to grasp for more of everything. The Apostle Paul describes such people: "And now, since they've lost all *natural* feelings, they have given themselves over to sensual, greedy, and reckless living. They stop at nothing to satisfy their impure appetites" (Ephesians 4:19).

4. Laziness – to avoid exertion: "Lazy people walk a path overgrown with thornbushes, but those with integrity travel a *wide,* level road" (Proverbs 15:19).

5. Wrath – an expression of intense indignation, anger, and rage. We are advised how to respond to such displays with the words, "A tender answer turns away rage, but a prickly reply spikes anger" (Proverbs 15:1).

6. Envy – a painful self-pity that longs to enjoy the benefits or advantages of another person. The Apostle Peter recommends a coping strategy: "So get rid of hatefulness and deception, of insincerity and jealousy and slander. Be like newborn babies, crying out for spiritual milk that will help you grow into salvation" (1 Peter 2:1-2).

7. Pride – an inordinate sense of self-esteem; thinking yourself superior to others. A wise man has observed, "Pride precedes destruction; an arrogant spirit gives way to a *nasty* fall" (Proverbs 16:18).

These sins are called "deadly" because of the observed consequences of pursuing any one of them, and Proverbs asserts they are detestable in God's opinion: "*Take note,* there are six things the Eternal hates; no, *make it* seven He abhors: [17]Eyes that look down on others, a tongue that can't be trusted, hands that shed innocent blood, [18]A heart that conceives evil plans, feet that sprint toward evil, [19]A false witness who breathes out lies, and anyone who stirs up trouble among the faithful" (Proverbs 6:16-19).

As I look at the "seven deadly myths" of *Ball*, I will do well to remember to look for things the Eternal may consider detestable.

1. *Ball* says the first deadly myth is that "straights know very little about homosexuality and would prefer to know even less" (5). The public is judged as living in complete denial concerning the sexuality of such famous persons as Rock Hudson and Liberace.

2. "There aren't many homosexuals in America" (13) is identified by *Ball* as a second myth, and in subsequent pages struggles to build a case that "at least 10% of the populace has demonstrated its homosexual proclivities so extensively that that proportion may reasonably be called 'gay'" (15), and cheerfully boasts that "gays make up a disproportionately large part—probably one third to one half—of the Catholic and Episcopalian clergy" (17). An interesting concept of morality is presented, that "when it comes to fighting the charge that *homosexuality is statistically abnormal hence immoral*, there is strength in numbers" (17). Here *Ball* portrays no moral compass, no sense that a thing may be intrinsically wrong regardless of public opinion or majority approval. The foundational reality portrayed in Genesis 18:32 shows the Creator, God, informing Abraham he intends to destroy the city of Sodom precisely because of the immoral behavior of the *vast majority* of its citizens. Abraham says, " Please don't be angry, Lord, *at my boldness.* Let me ask this just once more: suppose only 10 [righteous people] are found?" The Eternal One replies, "For the sake of only 10, I still will not destroy it," yet he does destroy the city and only one man and his two daughters (in whom the men of the city show no interest, and who obviously have no phobias regarding the homosexual city in which they have chosen to live) escape (see Genesis 19:1-22). Note the compassion of both Abraham and Lot toward the majority population despite blatant homosexual aggression against them, even to the point where the men of Sodom attempt to rape the messengers of God (Genesis 19:5).

3. "All gays are easy to spot" (18) is the third myth *Ball* seeks to dispel, arguing that in fact homosexuality is pervasive throughout the American population, and in a discussion of AIDS asserts that "the real infection spreading here is...homochondria" (26). I can't help noticing that name-calling, a form of psychological bullying, is habitual in *Ball*.

4. The myth that gays are victims of sin, insanity, and seduction is challenged with results of a 1979 public opinion survey by Roper indicating that 53% of respondents felt sexual orientation is determined entirely by environment (26). *Ball* takes issue with Jerry Falwell, Thomas Aquinas, the Vatican, "religious zealots" and many other naive straights and asserts that "sexual orientation usually is set at an early age and cannot be changed," linking it to racial identity with the remark that "to become a Negro is a weighty act," (32) thereby establishing a new myth in the claim that homosexual behavior is as genetic as race. *Ball* further argues that mental illness and gender confusion have little to do with homosexuality (32-40) and instead insists that "intimate contact with partners of the same sex is the ardent *first* choice of most homosexuals" (40). The fourth myth concludes with a section asserting that only "about 10% of all detected child molesters are gay" (43) and in general homosexuals are not recruited (45).

5. The myth that "gays are kinky, loathsome sex addicts" is bolstered by the claim that "most straights lump homosexuality into the 'creepy weirdo' class—alongside necrophilia, bestiality, pedophilia, feces fetishism, and snuff sex. To straights unused to thinking about such things, even the most conventional homosexual practices are shocking, sickening, ludicrous—in a word completely *perverse*" (46). This section describes these activities at length, admits that "there is more promiscuity among gays" (47), and laments that "our public image suggests that the gay experience consists of wanton promiscuity, not fidelity and bonding" (51), but the section mostly celebrates the "myth" than providing evidence to dispel it.

6. Anecdotal evidence is next offered to undermine the myth that "Gays are unproductive and untrustworthy members of society" (52) and complains that "the public's fearful perception of gay power is outlandishly inflated" (57), which seems to contradict the urgent message appearing previously that they easily constitute 10% of humanity.

7. *Ball* runs into trouble demythologizing a myth it identifies that "gays are suicidally unhappy because they are gay" (57) by noting "that it does have some basis in fact" (59) but blames these symptoms on the general persecution and estrangement that is their lot (59-61).

No correlation or contrast is attempted by *Ball* between the seven deadly sins and the seven deadly myths. As literature, *Ball* is disappointing shallow, and the section ends by observing that "what all seven have in common is their purpose, and combined effect, among heterosexuals: to rationalize an intense feeling of disapproval toward homosexuals and homosexuality" (61).

Ball next identifies three obstacles to acceptance of homosexuality: Sodomy laws preventing homosexual behavior (65-73), denying gays what are identified as the fundamental civil rights of marriage and parenthood (73-97), and public disapproval of gays (98-106). Some of the beliefs *Ball* would like to instill in my mind are as follows:

"Sexual feelings are not really chosen by anybody: homosexuality is just as healthy and natural for some persons as heterosexuality is for others. The sex and love lives of most gays and straights today are both similar and conventional. Gays would be as happy as anyone else, if we'd just treat them fairly. All sex acts among consenting adults [should be] decriminalized. Gays [should be] permitted all the standard rights of marriage and parenthood" (107-108). *Ball* concludes the chapter with the observation that "Our duty is to prod the body politic with a plan of deliberate stimuli, to hurry the change along" (109).

Ball's moral relativism functions as a blind spot. Driven by sexual passion, it cannot comprehend a life of obedience to Divine calling, or submission to a higher order than natural instincts. However, the things their "enemies" believe (mostly Christians) are not ideas that can fluctuate based on persuasion, propaganda, intimidation, name calling, or any other bullying technique.

Ball is not up against what I think or *feel* or *imagine* as true or *wish* were true. What matters here are eternal facts resulting in timeless beliefs that can't be shaken by political pull, social machinery, or propaganda campaign. Revelation from "God, the weaver of heaven and earth" (Psalm 134:3) compels me to believe that the term "marriage" has only one meaning and that is marriage sanctioned by God which joins one man and one woman in a single, exclusive union, as delineated in Scripture. From the beginning, God intended sexual intimacy to occur only between a man and a woman married to each other, and that they engage in no intimate sexual activity outside of that marriage. Any form of sexual activity including adultery, fornication, homosexuality, bisexual conduct, bestiality, and incest is a prideful act and offensive to God. No doubt pornography and attempts to change one's sex would also have made the ancient list had they been prominent or possible at the time.

Unable to comprehend absolute Truth, *Ball* is consequently unable to experience healing and escape from natural drives and cannot comprehend that God offers redemption and restoration to all who confess and forsake their sin, seeking His mercy and forgiveness through Jesus Christ. And without that experience *Ball* cannot treat the heterosexual world the way it longs to be treated by affording us compassion, love, kindness, respect, and dignity. Hateful and harassing behavior or attitudes directed toward any individual—including the ones exhibited by *Ball* toward me—are to be repudiated and are not in accord with Scripture nor the doctrines of the Church.

The reason to believe things explained in the Bible is not because they feel good or are easy, traditional, or safe. Believe them because they stand at the core of 6,000 years of salvation history and are unlikely to waiver in the face of the work *Ball* has cut out for itself in thinking to turn me into a convert.

It does intrigue me that *Ball* has almost succeeded in making me feel guilty about being heterosexual. I sense this would be a good time to let Os Guiness speak: "In our day, it is considered worse to judge evil than to do evil." *Ball* is mistaken in projecting the deception that it inhabits the moral high ground.

Chapter 2

The Roots of Homophobia and Homohatred

Now *Ball* wants to explore the mechanism of prejudice: what it isn't, what it is, and how it combines thought and emotion. The perspective is that human beings are mammals driven by two kinds of emotions: Tropic and counter-tropic emotions—the one defining good and happy feelings to be enjoyed, the other negative feelings to be avoided. In this context it is explained that prejudice evolved and was useful in primates for survival and reproductive advantage.

The point is that prejudice is a learned behavior, and therefore objections to homosexuality are nothing more than learned behavior, and therefore the agenda of the gay world is to gain acceptance through behavior modification—not of their own behavior, but of yours!

A dominant technique of *Ball* is to suggest that the most overt opponents of homosexuality have their own latent homosexual tendencies and are repressing their own instincts to act out homosexually. The intimidation factor behind this psychological manipulation is powerful. Have I ever been intrigued by the clothing and paraphernalia of the opposite sex? If so, it's because I'm really gay underneath it all! If a male tried on his older sister's lipstick when he was ten, it's because he was really gay. Was she a tomboy? Of course not—she was a lesbian! The implication is that any natural childhood curiosity is a mark of homosexuality and any passing same-sex attraction must be acted upon or I'm not being true to my animal self.

To build its case, *Ball* tells the story of Reverend Rose Mary Denman, "formerly strongly opposed to the ordination of gays as pastors, who one day awakened to her lesbianism, declared it, and was promptly defrocked" (127). *Ball* then breaks the "blueprinting of homohatred" into a seven-step sequence of stimuli and responses and illustrates its point with the story of "Billy Bigot" of "Redd's Neck, Arkansas," (134) and then reviews the success of various attempts by gays to end such prejudice with these strategies:

1. Argument to raise consciousness by lobbying legislators, lawyers, and any other public debate with the homohaters generally has not fully worked, but it has been somewhat effective—not to win the argument but to raise consciousness of the issues: "None of this is to say that argument has no place in propaganda; it can sometimes serve as an effective adjuvant to an essentially emotional appeal.... Even when argument seems effective, one rarely, if ever, actually persuades intellectually: rather, the appeal succeeds for emotional reasons" (137).

2. Fighting—storming the barricades—is evaluated as a dangerous and useless tactic because it has done "nothing whatever to improve straight America's picture of us" (141).

3. Shock tactics called "gender-bending" are decried as counterproductive and the proposed alternative is to "hammer in the wedge narrow end first.... Allow the camel's nose beneath your tent, and his whole body will soon follow" (146).

Three alternatives to the above tactics are proposed for "halting, derailing, or reversing the 'engine of prejudice'" (147):

1. Desensitization is the first proposed strategy for *Ball's* propaganda campaign: "to desensitize straights to gays and gayness, inundate them in a continuous flood of gay-related advertising, presented in the least offensive fashion possible. If straights can't shut off the shower, they may at least eventually get used to being wet" (149).

2. Jamming is a technique designed to create internal conflict in the minds of "bigots" by the use of associative conditioning and direct emotional modeling to achieve an "incompatible emotional response" so that "normal people feel *shame* when they are not thinking, feeling, or acting like one of the pack" (151). Shame on you for being intolerant of the growing social acceptance of homosexuality! *Ball* transcends morality for itself but wants you (and God) to feel naughty for that despicably judgmental attitude of yours: "The trick is to get the bigot into the position of feeling a conflicting twinge of shame" (151).

3. Conversion aims at getting the antigay bigots to actually like homosexuality. "By Conversion we actually mean something far more profoundly threatening to the American Way of Life, without which no truly sweeping social change can occur. We mean conversion of the average American's emotions, mind, and will, through a planned psychological attack, in the form of propaganda fed to the nation via the media" (153). *Ball* notes that "In Conversion, the bigot, who holds a very negative stereotypic picture, is repeatedly exposed to literal picture/label pairs, in magazines, and on billboards and TV, of gays— explicitly labeled as such!—who not only don't look like his picture of a homosexual, but are carefully selected to look either like the bigot and his friends, or like any one of his other stereotypes of all-right guys" (154).

Confident of its propaganda strategy, *Ball* concludes the chapter noting that "success depends, as always, on flooding the media. And that, in turn, means money, which means man-hours, which means unifying the gay community for a concerted effort," and that "those who aren't with us in this effort... are most decidedly against us" (157). Everyone who is not with them suffers from homophobia and homohate—animals needing psychological reconditioning.

In one breath *Ball* reacts violently to the idea that psychological reconditioning is either possible or desirable for a homosexual. In the next breath it devotes an entire chapter to proposing how such psychological reconditioning can and must be carried out against the entire heterosexual population.

Chapter 3

Strategy: Persuasion, not Invasion

"Good propaganda" is the agenda here, "a plan as manipulative as that which our enemies themselves employ. It's time to learn from Madison Avenue, to roll out the big guns. *Gays must launch a large-scale campaign—we've called it the Waging Peace campaign—to reach straights through the mainstream media.* We're talking about propaganda" (161).

The propaganda strategy is outlined as a mode of communication that first "relies more upon emotional manipulation than upon logic" (162), which explains why I have never respected or understood the gay campaign. I am a rational being created in the image of God and able to look with reason and discernment beyond desensitization, jamming, and conversion techniques of the gay propaganda machine.

Outright lies are discussed next, with warnings to be careful with these, because they are easily found out, on the one hand, yet "certain lies become hallowed public myths, persisting for as long as the public chooses to believe them" (163). Readers objecting to my assessment of *Ball* might suspect I am misrepresenting this book. In fact, I am merely summarizing major points. Now I will quote a full paragraph to reveal the underbelly of the movement:

> When, in a 1985 *Christopher Street* article, we presented a blueprint for a national propaganda effort, doubters derided the proposal as irrelevant or impotent, the methods as demeaning and fraudulent, and our intent as reactionary. In February 1988, however, a "war conference" of 175 leading gay activists, representing organizations from across the land, convened in Warrenton, Virginia, to establish a four-point agenda for the gay movement. The conference gave first priority to "a nation-wide media campaign to promote a positive image of gays and lesbians" (*Ball* 163).

No wonder I feel like I have a target drawn large on the back of my head. Someone has declared war on me, whether I believe it or not.

First of the four strategies is labeled "Come thou, Mountain, to Mohammed" which suggests that gays stop "trying to force-fit themselves into a straight mold... now it is the straights' turn to adjust.... Sooner or later, straights will be impressed by our gay pride, and come around" (164). Pride is at the heart of it all. Readers with a more comprehensive knowledge of salvation history will think back to another being who embraced Pride, an angel of light who fell like lightning from heaven.

The second strategy is branded, "I'd like to teach the world to sing" and suggests adopting "a sturdier code of ethics stressing maturity in love relationships, moderation in the pursuit of sex and other entertainments, sincerity and loving-kindness... for improving relations *within* the gay community, and only secondarily in reaching bigoted straights" (166).

Third, "come out, come out, wherever you are," which needs no explanation (167-170).

"Political conspiracies" is the fourth strategy for gay liberation: "Education (i.e., propaganda) and Politics (170). *Ball* does not underestimate the difficulty of this method and laments, "Time and again, religious conservatives have washed away our gains with a frothy tide of public outcry and backlash" (171) which I interpret as an invitation to respond sincerely to the core motives with something stronger than froth.

Next comes eight practical principles for persuasion which need no elaboration:

1. Don't just express yourself: communicate!
2. Seek ye not the saved nor the damned: appeal to the skeptics
3. Keep talking about gayness
4. Keep the message focused: You're a homosexual, not a whale
5. Portray gays as victims, not as aggressive challengers
6. Give potential protectors a just cause
7. Make gays look good
8. Make victimizers look bad (*Ball* 172-190).

Chapter 4

Tactics for Eating the Media Alive:
A Sound Bite Here, A Sound Bite There

Ball now advises gays to "develop a keen practical interest in the fine points of Public Relations, News Reporting, and Advertising—three media tactics whose arcane details interest only those in desperate need. But that includes you" (193).

If you have wondered how gay news seems to be covered in the media every day, it may well be due to the gay "waging peace campaign" which asserts that "gay news makes loud noise! Read all about it!" (194).

Tremendous progress is reported here, and *Ball* notes that "the sensation-hungry press has learned, bit by bit, to use the information resources our community offers" (195). At the same time, it advises against the gay pride marches which "tend to degenerate before the TV cameras into ghastly freak shows...and gender benders who think the mental health of uptight straight viewers is improved by visual shock therapy" (195). Recommended public relations suggestions go into considerable detail here, urging creative formatting, using news to make news, providing human interest and tout celebrity spokespersons (198).

This book predates social media but explores older forms of public relations including television, radio, magazines, newspapers, and "outdoor" (billboards, subway posters, etc.). Television is *Bell's* first choice for its graphic and intrusive qualities, radio is not to be neglected, magazines should be used because such reading is a solitary pastime and readers are likely to pay closer attention, and newspapers are esteemed of marginal value but still somewhat useful.

The right message on a billboard—carefully designed and targeted—can sway an entire community of passers-by (199-204). Recommended ads are included here, such as "In Russia, they tell you what to be. In America, we have the freedom to be ourselves...and to be the best—*the National Gay & Lesbian Community proudly joins America in celebrating July 4*" (207).

Do not fail to notice the Soviet-style propaganda tactics being employed here by a so-called "community" that has declared "war" as they use this very ad to "tell you what to be."

It's Tuesday, January 27, and I'm at a journalism conference at Hillsdale College where I just had a fascinating conversation with radio talk show host, lawyer, and veteran of all things political Hugh Hewitt. He has spoken on the topic, "Why Conservatives Dominate Talk Radio" and offered the assessment that these pundits "really know about what they're speaking, and they are not trying to trick you."

As a journalism professor, I appreciated the five challenges he outlined for those in my profession: Teach them to be good, teach them to be gracious, teach them to be grateful (and able to name their mentors), teach them to work very hard, and believe in your heart that if we lose, the country loses: "We are America's last best hope."

After his presentation I told him I was reading *Ball* 26 years too late and wondered out loud how the gay agenda has succeeded so well given its deliberate trickery and manipulative marketing strategies—the exact opposite of the gracious ways he has just outlined for talk radio.

He replied, "Do you know anyone who has died of AIDS? Do you know anyone who is gay?" Of course, the answer to both questions is yes, but notice that instead of answering my question, he came back with an emotional response, not a logical or rational one. Knowing someone who does a certain behavior has no logical connection to whether that behavior is right or wrong. Notice that even a very gifted and witty and *conservative* talk show host is unwittingly parroting the propaganda you've just read about that has been deliberately planted in the America media over the past few decades.

I asked for a further explanation and he said, "Young people today don't care about that issue any more." In other words, the gay propaganda has been a success. By "young people" he meant the college students we were surrounded with at that moment born into a pro-gay propaganda-saturated media.

I mentioned that taking a carefully reasoned conversation to its conclusion is an ongoing challenge when conversing with young people steeped in logical fallacies and distracted sound bites. Now, understand that Hugh is an extremely smart and seasoned lawyer, professor of law, former employee of President Reagan, and a savvy journalist, so I said,

"What is the story-behind-the-story of gay acceptance in our culture?"

"Rob Bell," he said, identifying the former evangelical pastor and author of the 2011book *Love Wins* as a model of the theological and spiritual problem of our time. And then Hugh put it all together for me in his concise and perceptive way: "They stopped believing in hell" (personal interview, Jan. 27, 2015).

I have said to the Sunday school class I teach, "For the Church to ordain gays is the heresy of the 21st century." What is heresy? For a Greek citizen to worship at the temple of the fertility goddess Aphrodite is not heresy but just a pagan practice. However, for the Church to encourage the same activity and perhaps associate Aphrodite with the Holy Spirit—that would be heresy.

For a "Supreme Court" of some Western nation in the 21st century to sanction homosexual marriage is not heresy but just a pagan practice. However, for the Church to ordain a homosexual and proclaim same-sex marriage as sanctioned by God—that would be heresy.

Gay marriage and ordaining of homosexuals is a symptom of the larger heresy of Universalism: We've stopped believing in hell. A wide swath of the Church has stopped reading and understanding and accurately interpreting scripture. Our culture has embraced its own story; we have forgotten God's story. Our culture looks from a very narrowly human-gratification point of view; we have lost awareness of God's point of view.

If *God* is the Logos, the Word, the Voice, the Author of Reason and Absolute Truth, it stands to reason that a people who abandon Him are doomed to an irrational relativism. If there were no God, it would be an excusable stew in which to find ourselves; given what can be known about the God who is, the irrational relativism is an inexcusable deception coming down from the father of lies.

The word "lies" brings me back to page 209 where *Ball* is talking about the value of using Public Service Announcements (PSAs) for getting out their message. Call this number if you've been attacked for being gay, etc. They warn, "Don't show even the mildest homoeroticism." Rather, "try a more oblique approach, one that makes refusal [of stations] to air our PSAs look unreasonable, possibly illegal, and patently bigoted" (211). *Ball* notes that "AIDS-related support groups may be the first to win airtime. For our money, however, we'd rather see ads for gay antiviolence projects, hotlines, counseling groups, senior citizens' homes, runaway-shelters" etc. (211).

Ball's next scheme, way back in 1989, was "to run symbolic gay candidates for every high political office." Page 212 reads, "When all else fails, homosexuality for president." The current American president fulfills its wildest dreams.

Ball's next recommendation: "The gloves come off," followed by a 30-page portfolio of pro-gay advertising (215-245) including such things as "Adolf Hitler: Madman. Murderer. Homophobe." And here is a picture of someone in a white KKK robe and the text, "Some guys have trouble accepting gay people."

All that's from the book in my left hand. The book in my right hand reads, "Think, brainless people; stupid people, when will you get it? Does the God who set the ear *in its place* not hear? Does the God who made the eye not see? Does the God who teaches the nations and guides humanity to knowledge, not exercise *just* correction? The Eternal knows the *highest* thoughts of the wise, and they are worthless" (Psalm 94:8-11).

Question: If *Ball* brands me as a homohater now, what would it think if I actually used the tactics against it that it is using against me?

Chapter 5

Getting our Act(ivists) Together:
Unity, Organization Fundraising

This chapter complains that "the gay kingdom is disorganized" with "too many fiefdoms" (248) and needs to organize into one universally known national gay organization with "coordinated task forces dedicated to political lobbying, legal action, gay life, health issues, and public education" (249), taking lessons from trade unions such as the AFL-CIO.

A unified identity is promoted where "homosexual as gays" will be the big paradigm shift. *Ball* identifies "the social chasm between homosexual males and females who... insist upon separate names: 'gay men' and 'lesbians'" (257). It further identifies among the male population the "R-types" who can often pass for straight and the "Q-types" or "homosexuals on display" (258). The point is made that "R's dominate the sexual hierarchy of the gay male world, while Q's dominate its political hierarchy" (259).

"The new gay televangelism" suggests that "a gay media campaign can do wondrous spiritual—and then financial—things to our torpid community," a process that resembles "a religious conversion" (263). This must be followed by a national fundraising program that involves "Name, Mission, Tax Deductibility, and a Good Ladder" (264). The bottom rung of this ladder is "harmonic convergence" and climbs through "handout, advertisement, news item, brochure newsletter, mass-produced letter, typewritten letter, handwritten letter, telephone conversation, large group discussion, small group discussion, one-to-one conversion," and at the top of the ladder is "hypnotic suggestion" (266). The strategy is to achieve all this with government grants, foundation grants, business contributions, and individual contributions.

My impression for the past couple decades has been that America has in fact been under the stupor of gay hypnotic suggestion. I have just now discovered that it is real, it is deliberate, and the main people with intellectual, emotional, and spiritual immunity are those with strong religious convictions such as Muslims, Mormons, Jews, and Bible-believing Christ followers. Success for *Ball* is not yet complete. The most stubborn brain-washing candidates have been saved for last.

Chapter 6

Gay Pride Goeth Before a Fall

"This chapter will tell you what's wrong with a lot of gays, why it's wrong, and how you can dance the new steps . . . after the ball" (276). The ten steps below are called "ten misbehaviors" and are based on a fascinatingly confused definition of "wrong" and the virtues from which it derives a sense of what is "right" in a world devoid of established moral codes.

Step one of the ball dance is to recognize the "Lies, lies, all lies!" of the straight world that prevent young people from openly embracing any homosexual inclinations they may have and spends ten pages lamenting the stories of people with same-sex attractions who fail to give in to the temptations they experience.

Step two of the ball dance, called "The Rejection of Morality" quotes Oscar Wilde who said, "the only way to get rid of temptation is to yield to it" (289).

Ball only recognizes two alternatives for the person with a same sex attraction. "He can (1) accept the received values of conventional morality and hate himself, or (2) step outside the conventional way of looking at things, begin to think for himself and form his own values, realize that the Judeo-Christian prejudice against homosexuality is arbitrary, absurd, and evil, and, by rejecting it, replace his self-hatred with self-esteem" (290). *Ball* writes that "many—we hope most—gays eventually reach this stage of maturity" (290).

Gay readers should note the "either-or" logical fallacy in the above paragraph. The two options identified are not your only choices. You can accept conventional morality and not hate yourself by instead repenting of the hateful thing about yourself and sacrificing it on the altar of obedience to the God who made you and loves you. This act places you in the company of all those who in response to the grace of God see their shame replaced by honor, their guilt replaced by innocence, their fear overcome by the power of God.

Note also that in this paragraph *Ball* reaches new levels, not of heterophobia, of the demonic blathering of those cast out of heaven and spewing Divinityphobia. Pride indeed went before Lucifer, the Angel of Light who was tossed out of heaven, and nowhere have I seen it more explicitly stated by gays that homosexual behavior is the demonic substitute of God's created order.

My gay roommate in college confessed to Satan worship and participation in various occult practices. At that time I asked whether perhaps his homosexuality was not a symptom rather than the disease. He said that due to life-threatening experiences in his spiritism practices, he had left that behind, but his interest in homosexuality had a stronger grip on him that he was unwilling to address.

It only makes sense. For every virtue, the enemy of God has introduced a vice: For humility he substitutes pride, for kindness—envy, for self-control—gluttony, for chastity—lust and pornography, for patience—anger, for liberality—greed, and for diligence—sloth.

Likewise, *Ball* reveals a mentality that counterfeits the seven classical virtue, valuing doubt over faith, despair over hope, hate over love, war over peace, confusion over logic, insanity over sanity, and foolishness over wisdom.

Carve God out of your heart and you'll replace Him with astonishing filth and stupidity as evidenced by *Ball's* observations that "many gays choose to live without morality" (292) and humbly acknowledges, "we are as much adherents of Hedonism as those we decry—but (we hope) at a higher and kinder level" (295).

Step three of the ball dance is about "Narcissism and Self-centered Behavior" and acknowledges that "rejecting morality leads to susceptibility to a personality disorder" (295). The "morality" *Ball* aspires to includes a recommendation to "practice safe sex" and "contribute money for the good of the gay community" (299).

Step four of the ball dance on "Self-Indulgence, Self-Destruction" decries the rejection of morality leading to the sentiment, "It's our orgy, and we'll die if we want to" (302). This section decries the self-indulgence of the fast-lane lifestyle, drug use, raunchy and aggressive sex, and begs the gay world to instead adopt "moderation and service," the values of straight society (306).

Step five of the ball dance is on "Indulging Our Privates In Public" and discourages open homosexual intercourse in public places and goes into explicit detail describing and elaborating on these behaviors while suggesting to avoid them. Doublespeak—a propaganda technique of <u>pre</u>tending to say one thing while <u>in</u>tending the opposite—is rampant in *Ball.*

Step six of the ball dance, "Misbehavior in Bars," is equally crude and makes it plain that the working homosexual definition of "morality" is essentially anything that results in bad public relations.

Step seven of the ball dance deplores "Misbehavior in Relationships" and observes that a root of the problem is that "relationships between gay men don't usually last very long," and this is partly "due to the characteristics of male physiology and psychology, which make the sexual and romantic pairing of man with man inherently less stable than the pairing of man with woman" (318). Long-term love is scarce for these men, but they should not exacerbate their problem with misbehavior.

Step eight of the ball dance explores the "Emotional Blockage and Anesthesia" of something called "Shrill Doll Syndrome, a.k.a. Tussaud's Disease" in which a person holds his body "tensely and rigidly, in an unnatural posture reminiscent of department store mannequins (which are usually designed by gay men)" (332). The frigid physical posture reflects a frigid emotional posture, and *Ball* congratulates itself for writing this section by concluding, "If even one reader takes our plea to heart and seeks help, whether within himself or in a psychiatrist's office, for his emotional frigidity or his alcoholism or drug addiction, the depressing task of writing this chapter will have been 100% worthwhile" (337).

Step nine of the ball dance ponders "Reality-Denial, Nonsensical Thinking, and Mythomania," mental activities, wishful thinking, and coping mechanisms that gays engage in at their peril when they should instead be embracing facts and logic. I admire the sentiment while experiencing astonishment at the absence of logic portrayed here.

Step ten of the ball dance is on "Gay Political Fascism and the Oppression of P.C." and suggests that most of the literature in the 20 years prior to the publication of *Ball* has harmed rather than advanced the gay cause.

Having established the new gay moral code of what not to do—the ten misbehaviors that have hurt the gay cause, we now enter an *After the Ball* era where the objective is "to suggest a new, self-policing social code for the gay community, and a new plan for the structuring of that community's 'family' life" (357). I am intrigued that *Ball's* "Self-Policing Social Code" is at once incredibly complex compared to something like the Ten Commandments and yet ridiculously focused on one narrow aspect of human identity—sexuality.

The first seven rules are for relating to straight people, beginning with "I won't have sex in public places," and touches on "If I'm a pederast or a Sadomasochist, I'll keep it under wraps" (360).

The next eight rules are for relating to other gays, beginning with "I won't lie" and includes, "I'll drop my search for Mr. Right and settle for what's realistic." While *Ball* is utterly weighted down with its own lies, name-calling, and crudity, yet in its own self-policing social code it admonishes, "I won't re-enact straight oppression by name-calling and shouting down..." (360). Self-policing is off to a very bad start.

The final seven rules are for relating to yourself, beginning with "I'll stop trying to be eighteen forever," "I won't have more than two alcoholic drinks a day," and "I'll listen to common sense, not emotion" (360). I've read a lot of literature over the years, but I've never seen thicker irony—these absurdly detailed rules coming from *Ball* which claims elsewhere to be so utterly devoted to "liberation." Remember here that one author of *Ball* is a Harvard educated logician; the other *Ball* is devoted to public persuasion tactics, and their combined issue spurts profoundly illogical and unseemly pus.

The very next page of *Ball* attacks the "idiotic misconceptions" of "gay pundits" as it seeks to get "Back to Plato: A modest proposal to resurrect the 'traditional family'" (361). The page that follows laments the problems gays have in "forging lasting friendships with their own narcissistic, bitchy, rejecting kind" (363).

Ball acknowledges that "the gay community has no generation-to-generation continuity" (364) and attributes this "wretched situation" to "the complete absence, in the gay lifestyle, of anything corresponding to family" (365).

The family model put forward (here's where Plato comes in) is of an ancient Greek scenario where a male of age 30 or so (*erastes*—the adult lover) would become the mentor and adult role model of a youth of 17 or so (*eromenos*—the beloved) in "an alliance partaking equally of the qualities of father-son, teacher-student, and big brother-little brother relationships... with the superadded bond of explicitly sexual love" (367).

Ball suggests that in the normal course of events the youth would marry, sire children, and in his adulthood perhaps establish "a fresh alliance, in turn, with a younger male" (368).

This is the envisioned future of gay marriage in America—a state-recognized system for a self-perpetuating institution of homosexuality. Honestly, what did you *think* was going on when gays adopt children?

Ball recognizes such families as an urgent matter because "the gay population is... getting older" and "if we wish to resurrect the 'traditional gay family,' we must provide suitable incentives" (370). A couple pages of details and explanations are offered, followed by another ironic disclaimer: "To a dirty mind, nothing is clean. We go on record, here and now, as stating explicitly that we do not advocate adults having sex with minors under any circumstances whatever" (372).

At this point, readers with even a vague trace of intelligence are bound to ask of *Ball*, "If your disclaimer is true, then exactly what was it you were advocating on the previous 12 pages?" Its attempt at an answer comes in a one paragraph statement that if homosexuals are to gain their rights, then they must also accept their responsibilities (373).

Chapter 7

Jumping to Conclusions

The closing section of *Ball* calls on homosexuals to "Go home and make a decision" (376). The choice is to be either vigilant or complacent, and readers are advised, "Think of your vigilance as a sort of condom worn to prevent infection with totalitarianism" (378).

The text then revisits its agenda that anticipates a world where "it simply doesn't occur to anyone that there's anything more unusual about being gay than about preferring praline ice cream to double Dutch chocolate," and where *everyone* believes gayness is "a valid and healthy condition" (379). And this: "We want... to revoke all laws criminalizing sex acts" (380).

The concluding paragraph informs me that the ball *is* over: "The masks have come off,... Tomorrow, the real gay revolution begins. So go home, get changed, and be at the station by eight" (383).

Chapter 8

Considerations

I wasn't at the ball, so I never saw the masks come off. But they are indeed gone. America looks gay today, and if you question that bias, turn the TV to any channel and see if that belief isn't reinforced every ten minutes or so. A program without a gay character rarely gets air time. A newscast without gay references is seldom scripted. *Ball's* propaganda campaign has succeeded, probably beyond its fondest hopes and dreams.

Tactically speaking, it was a brilliant success. The idea of a free market place of thought was built into the founding documents of the United States and was expressed by Thomas Jefferson (3rd United States President) in a letter to a friend in 1787. He wrote, "I am persuaded that the good sense of the people will always be found to be the best army. They may be led astray for a moment, but will soon correct themselves."

The question to ponder now is whether gay marriage truly reflects the good sense of the people. And if not, what will "the people" do? Whether the current push for gay marriage "will soon correct" itself seems unlikely, for in this instance we have not just competing ideologies, but a deviously crafted propaganda campaign waged by an influential and wealthy special interest group accompanied by complicity with both the executive and judiciary branches of the federal government. "Gay rape of American public opinion" is not too strong a way to state what has happened in the 21st century.

In writing this review of *Ball* it was difficult to hide my astonishment at both the moral depravity and profound ignorance of its authors given their academic pedigrees, for the book is shabbily written, filthy in thought, word, and deed, pathetically illogical. And yet—in spite of B*all's* deplorable and untenable stance—it has succeeded magically as the gay manifesto needed to transform America into moral bankruptcy.

Nothing is new in all this, and the solution to all the longings of the homosexual population were long ago addressed in the very book *Ball* so violently opposes. John, the close friend of Jesus, lovingly addresses the big gay lie that claims homosexual behavior is normal and should be acceptable:

> If we go around bragging, "We have no sin," then we are fooling ourselves and are strangers to the truth. [9]But if we own up to our sins, God shows that He is faithful and just by forgiving us of our sins and purifying us from the pollution of all the bad things we have done. [10]If we say, "We have not sinned," then we depict God as a liar and *show that* we have not let His word find its way into our hearts. (1 John 1:8-10)

The same text clearly explains the alternative to homosexual and any other sinful lifestyle:

> Everyone who lives a life of habitual sin is living in moral anarchy. That's what sin is. [5]You realize that He came to eradicate sins, that there is not the slightest bit of sin in Him. [6]The ones who live in *an intimate relationship with* Him do not persist in sin, but anyone who persists in sin has not seen and does not know the real Jesus.
>
> [7]Children, don't let anyone pull one over on you. The one doing the right thing is just imitating Jesus, the Righteous One.
>
> [8]The one persisting in sin belongs to the diabolical one, who has been all about sin from

the beginning. That is why the Son of God came into our world: to destroy the plague of destruction inflicted *on the world* by the diabolical one.

⁹Everyone who has been born into God's family avoids sin *as a lifestyle* because the genes of God's children come from God Himself. Therefore, a child of God can't live a life of persistent sin. (1 John 3:4-9)

No further clarification should be necessary in supporting my observation that for the Church to ordain gay clergy or permit members to persist in homosexual practices constitutes a heresy of some magnitude. At the same time, the Church must lovingly embrace and nurture individuals who experience same-sex attractions but are waging spiritual warfare against these evils the same as does the heterosexual who must fight sexual temptation.

Everyone has some cross to bear, some form of sin that comes easily. The essence of the Godly life is the daily practice of transcending whatever that temptation may be whether that person be an alcoholic, swindler, liar, or exhibits any other quality condemned by scripture as sinful. Sadly, *Ball* utterly rejects such grace or even the need for such grace.

Yet grace from God abounds to anyone who acknowledges a behavior as sin and repents.

Jefferson wrote in the same letter mentioned earlier, "Were it left to me to decide whether we should have a government without newspapers, or newspapers without a government, I should not hesitate a moment to prefer the latter." By "newspapers" he meant a free press.

Do we have a free press in America today? The heavy media bias favoring the homosexual agenda suggests that either the press is no longer free, or people like myself are unable to adequately express their views, don't care enough to give it the needed effort, or don't believe addressing the issue can make any difference. We are where *Ball* said the homosexual cause was back in 1989—impotent.

Helpless is precisely what *Ball* wants me to feel, and frankly, that is how I felt, ignoring the issue as long as homosexual behavior was a strictly secular issue in a morally bankrupt society spiraling rapidly and probably unstoppably downward. I just shrugged and enjoyed an ultimate confidence I feel from such Scriptures as this:

> For wickedness will not *get the upper hand*; *it shall not* rule the land where righteous people

live lest good people go bad and do what is
wrong. [4]Be good, Eternal One, to those who are
good, to those who are filled with integrity. [5]The
Eternal will send all the wicked away along with
those who *pervert what's good and* twist it in
their own crooked way. (Psalm 125:3-5)

But now I see churches embracing and propagating
this lie. That hits too close to home. I wonder if
perhaps God doesn't always act alone in sending the
wicked away. Perhaps he will use my influence and
the strength of others who would prefer to live by the
Ten Commandments rather than by the homosexual,
22-point "Self-Policing Social Code" to turn the
country from wickedness to righteousness.

It has happened before—twice before. They
were called Great Awakenings, and a Third Great
Awakening may be our best, last hope—lest the
Almighty come (yet again) to smite the land with a
curse.

I dreamed last night that I lived in an
astonishingly magnificent home, massive, with
leaded windows and many, many ornately decorated
rooms. I did not know most of the other people living
in the house, but I did notice that the house was on
fire. Live coals smoldered in the floor between the

joists and I sensed the building would soon erupt in an inferno or simply collapse as hot coals ate away the supports.

The ornate and richly woven carpet was becoming threadbare from the bottom up, and I would not step on it for fear of getting burned while falling through the ceiling of the room below. I glanced around in search of a plan, and there I saw an elderly servant woman dressed in black with a white apron. She was the only other person who noticed the fire, and together we poured tea cups of cold water into the blue-hot flames.

Now it's the morning of February 8, 2015, and I can report that last night, before the dream, I attended the musical *Godspell* performed by Jesus and his twelve disciples—many of them students of mine. Judas was double-cast as John the Baptist who stood in the aisle just inches away from where I sat. I found myself weeping as he—in pure and powerful tones—delivered the opening rendition of "Prepare Ye the Way of the Lord."

Thank you, Michael. You are named after the archangel, and in your conflicted role as both John the Baptist and Judas, you are commissioned to both work out your own salvation in fear and trembling even as you do the Lord's preparation work. The Commander of the Lord's Army will sustain you.

The average age of last night's cast was around 20 and in their lifetimes the concept of gay marriage has gone from being perceived by the masses as a bizarre social construct that has never succeeded anywhere in the history of civilization to becoming not only the law of the land, but the great heresy of many 21st century churches.

I cannot ignore the heavenly vision, so I have thrown my window open, have stuck my head out, and am shouting to anyone who will listen, "I'm mad as heaven and I won't take it anymore. Gay rape of the public is one thing; gay rape of the Body of Jesus Christ (the Church) is pushing a red button with consequences beyond your comprehension.

"Repent, turn from your wicked ways, abandon your pride of worshiping yourself as god, and just watch and see the astonishing actualization that can transpire in your life when you abandon your will to God, invite him to control your life, and devote your energies toward becoming all that you were created to be rather than following your lower instincts and becoming twisted into all that the Un-creator longs to un-make of you.

"An upward path and a downward path lie before you. Whether you believe it today or wait to experience it later, the alternative to the upward path of repentance and obedience is the downward path prophesied to end with the devil and his angels in a lake of fire (prepared by God in his all-knowing comprehension of best practices) to eradicate evil and make the coming new world a safe place for the holiness without which no person will see God."

Part of the actual prophesy reads as follows:

It is done! I am the Alpha and the Omega, the beginning and the end. I will see to it that the thirsty drink freely from the fountain of the water of life. [7]To the victors will go this inheritance: I will be their God, and they will be My children. [8]*It will not be so* for the cowards, the faithless, the sacrilegious, the murderers, the sexually immoral, the sorcerers, the idolaters, and all those who deal in deception. They will inherit *an eternity in* the lake that burns with fire and sulfur, which is the second death. (Revelation 21:6-8)

Notice that cowards are mixed right in there with homosexuals in fuel for the lake of fire, so I set aside my cowardice and publish this essay.

Paul, a Jewish scholar I admire, wrote something that puts the entire issue of homosexuality into proper context, including instructions on how to overcome this—or any other—temptation:

It's clear that our flesh entices us into practicing some of its most heinous acts: participating in corrupt sexual relationships, impurity, unbridled lust, 20idolatry, witchcraft, hatred, arguing, jealousy, anger, selfishness, contentiousness, division, 21envy *of others' good fortune,* drunkenness, drunken revelry, and other shameful vices *that plague humankind.* I told you this clearly before, and I only tell you again *so there is no room for confusion:* those who give in to these ways will not inherit the kingdom of God.

22The Holy Spirit produces a different kind of fruit: *unconditional* love, joy, peace, patience, kindheartedness, goodness, faithfulness, 23gentleness, and self-control. You won't find any law opposed to fruit like this. 24Those of us who belong to the Anointed One have crucified our old lives and put to death the flesh and all the lusts and desires that plague us. (Galatians 5:19-24)

A legitimate prayer in these times is that a great spiritual awakening will sweep over America that would provide for us a tiny taste of that coming Kingdom when the will of God will be done on earth just as it is done in heaven.

An important detail of this prayer will be to pray against Belial. Do as I did when I walked around my house, my neighborhood, my workplace, and my church praying against the demon Belial. I prayed to cast it out of each place, and I set a spiritual hedge around those properties so that Belial will have no influence here, and that people who enter these places will be freed from its lies. (The pronoun "it" refers to "Belial" as it is a fallen demon without race or gender.)

How is praying against Belial significant? Christ followers have been given authority to cast out demons, and this is the only power by which the invasion of the demonic into the Church can be held in check.

Why pray against Belial in particular? Because it is an extremely powerful demon tasked with advancing homosexual behavior throughout the world. The Hebrew term *belial* is translated "worthless" or "without value" and appears 27 times in the Hebrew Scriptures, 15 times to indicate worthless people including idolaters (Deut. 13:13), the homosexual men of Gibeah (Judges 19:22, 20:13), and Nabal, and Shimei, the sexually perverted sons of Eli (1 Samuel 2:12).

New Testament instructions on dealing with Belial are explicit:

> Don't develop partnerships with those who are not followers of Jesus' teachings. For what real connection can exist between righteousness and rebellion? How can light participate in darkness? What harmony can exist between the Anointed and Belial? Do the faithful and the faithless have anything in common? Can the temple of God find common ground with idols? Don't you see that we house the temple of the living God within us? *Remember when* He said, "I will make My home with them and walk among them. I will be their God, and they will be My people. So then turn away from them, turn away and leave *without looking back*," says the Lord. "Stay away from anything unclean, *anything impure,* and I will welcome you. And I will be for you as a father, and you will be for Me as sons and daughters," says the Lord Almighty! (2 Cor. 6:14-18)

The Supreme Court has no spiritual authority over Belial, and neither do organizations once branded "church" that ordain gay clergy and perform "marriages" for homosexuals. They have lost their way.

So have those who are so afraid of losing their jobs that they refuse to stand up for what they know to be right and have allowed the gay mafia to trade places with them in the closet.

Belial is winning America in spite of its small hard core constituency precisely because it is a spiritual power stronger than anything except the Holy Spirit and that powerful messenger of God, Michael, and his holy ones who fight on behalf of the holiness without which no one will see God.

Come out of your closet now so you can be used of God to save your gay relatives and friends from the destruction set for them at the hand of Belial. Pray against Belial in all the places where you live, work, and play so that you will live to see the day prophesied by Isaiah: They will say of Me, "Only by the Eternal One *shall I see things through. Only by God* shall I go with integrity and strength *through life*." Now all those who burned with anger against God will come to Him and be shamed (Isaiah 45:24).

Due to my confidence that the above prayer will indeed be answered, "I wait for the Eternal—my soul awaits rescue—and I put my hope in His transforming word. My soul waits for the Lord to break into the world more than night watchmen expect the break of day, even more than night watchmen expect the break of day" (Psalm 130:5-6).

Jesus told Pilate, "My kingdom is not in this physical realm" (John 18:36), yet it has penetrated every major culture on Earth regardless of political opposition. So it's clear to me that the Supreme Court decision regarding gay marriage is of no consequence to the true Church throughout the world which will maintain the same marriage stance it has held for 2000 years—though the issue will clearly separate sheep from goats.

As for the future of America, that is up to you. May the scales fall from your eyes to see and understand the gay revolution for what it truly is. And if you wish to stand against it, my feeling is that prayer is your most effective weapon.

Appendix
Explicit Biblical References to Homosexuality

Genesis 19:1-13

The two heavenly messengers arrived in Sodom that evening, and Lot was sitting at the gate of the city. When Lot saw them, he went out to meet them and bowed low, his face touching the ground.

Lot: 2 Please, my lords, take time to come into your servant's house to spend the night and wash your feet. Then you can rise early and be on your way.

Messengers: No, we will be *fine* spending the night in the city square.

3 But Lot persisted *and urged them to come home with him and enjoy his hospitality*. They agreed finally and came with Lot to his house. Lot prepared a huge meal for them, served with unleavened bread, and they ate *until they were full*. 4 But before they could lie down *to rest for the night*, the men of the city—that is, the men of Sodom, young and old alike, every last one of them—surrounded the house 5 and called out to Lot.

Men of Sodom: Where are the men who came *with you* to your house tonight? *We saw them go in with you!* Bring them out here. We want to have sex with them!

6 Lot slipped out of the door to address the men, shutting it *firmly* behind him.

Lot: 7 *Look,* I beg you, brothers, don't do this. Don't sink to this level of depravity! 8 Look—I have two daughters. Both are virgins. How about this: I'll bring them out for you instead. You can do with them as you please. But please don't do anything to these men. They are my guests. They deserve the protection of my home.

Lot leaves the safety of his home to negotiate with the men of the city, all of whom seem determined to have sex with his guests. Al though his courage is commend able, his solution is deplorable—offering his virgin daughters for the deviant pleasures of his neighbors. But Lot knows their sexual preference is for his guests, not his daughters; so the offer is safe, and he has bought some time.

Men of Sodom: 9 Get out of the way, man!

(to each other) Look, this guy came to our city as a stranger. *He's not one of us,* and yet he thinks he has the right to judge *all of us*!

(to Lot) *You better watch out, or* we'll treat you far worse than we will your guests!

They came at Lot and pushed him hard against the door until it was about to break. ¹⁰ Just then the men inside reached out and pulled Lot into the house with them, shutting the door *securely to block the men of Sodom out.* ¹¹ Then the *heavenly* messengers struck all of the men pressing at the door with blindness—both young and old alike. *It wasn't long before* they exhausted themselves *blindly* groping for the door.

Messengers *(to Lot):* ¹² Do you have anyone else here in the city—sons-in-law, sons, daughters, or any other members of your family—*whom you want to save?* If so, you need to get them out of here right now! ¹³ We are going to destroy this place. Because of the immense outcry the Eternal One has received regarding the depravity of this city, the Eternal has sent us here to destroy it.

Judges 19:17-28

Old Man: Where are you going? Where are you from?

Levite: ¹⁸ We are traveling from Bethlehem in Judah to the far parts of the hill country of Ephraim. I went to Bethlehem in Judah, and I am returning to my home. No one yet has offered us hospitality. ¹⁹ We, your servants, have straw and food for the donkeys, and we also have bread and wine, enough for me, my mistress, and my young servant. We don't require anything else.

Old Man: 20 Peace be with you. I will take care of everything you need, but do not spend the night in the square.

21 The old man took them home and fed their donkeys. They washed *the dust of the road from* their feet, ate, and drank. 22 While they were eating and drinking, the men of the city, an evil assembly, surrounded the house and began beating on the door. They called to the owner.

Men of the City: Bring out *your guest,* the man whom you have welcomed into your house. We want to have sexual relations with him!

Old Man *(pleading with them)*: 23 I beg you. Don't do this wicked thing to the traveler I have welcomed into my care. 24 I have a virgin daughter, and this man has a mistress. I will bring them out to you to do what you want with them, but don't dishonor my guest with your wickedness.

25 The men would not listen. At last the Levite seized his mistress and pushed her outside. They raped her repeatedly and abused her all night long until the sun

came up, when they left her alone. 26 Then the woman crept to the doorway of the house where her master had spent the night. She collapsed and lay there as the sun rose in the sky. 27 Her master, at last, woke and rose; and when he went to the door to prepare to go on his way, there was his mistress, lying near the doorway, her hands on the threshold.

Levite: 28 Get up. It's time for us to go.

But she could not answer him. He put her body on the donkey and set out for home.

Leviticus 18:21-27 God's Instructions to Moses

21 Do not sacrifice your children to Molech. Such *an unholy sacrifice* desecrates your God's name. I am *your God,* the Eternal One. 22 You are not to have sexual relations with a man in the same way you do with a woman; such a thing is detestable. 23 Do not engage in a sexual act with an animal—this includes men as well as women; such behavior defiles you and perverts the proper order of things.

24 Do not defile yourselves by engaging in any of these *perverse* things. I am driving out all these other nations ahead of you because they have corrupted themselves *with disgusting acts like these.* 25 The

entire land *of Canaan* is so impure that I will punish the land until it vomits out those who dwell upon it. 26 I want you to keep My decrees and judgments. No Israelite and no outsider living among you should commit any of the detestable acts that 27 the people who were in Canaan before you committed when they desecrated the land.

Leviticus 20:13-16

13 If a man has sexual relations with another man, they have participated in a detestable act. Both men are to be put to death, for their blood is on them. 14 Any man who marries a woman and her mother commits a depraved act. He and both women are to be burned to death so that such depravity will not exist in the community. 15 Any man who engages in a sexual act with an animal is to be put to death along with the animal. 16 Any woman who approaches an animal to engage in some sexual act must be put to death along with the animal, for their blood is on them.

Romans 1: 18-27

18 For the wrath of God is breaking through from heaven, opposing all *manifestations of* ungodliness and wickedness by the people who do wrong to keep

God's truth in check. [19] These people are not ignorant about what can be known of God, because He has shown it to them *with great clarity*. [20] From the beginning, creation in its magnificence enlightens us to His nature. Creation itself makes His undying power and divine identity clear, even though they are invisible; and it voids the excuses *and ignorant claims* of these people [21] because, despite the fact that they knew the one true God, they have failed to show the *love,* honor, and appreciation due to the One who created them! Instead, their lives are consumed by vain thoughts that poison their foolish hearts. [22] They claim to be wise; but they have been exposed as fools, *frauds, and con artists*— [23] only a fool would trade the splendor and beauty of the immortal God to worship images of the common man or woman, bird or reptile, or *the next* beast *that tromps along.*

[24] So God gave them just what their lustful hearts desired. *As a result,* they violated their bodies and invited shame into their lives. [25] *How?* By choosing a foolish lie over God's truth. They gave their lives and devotion to the creature rather than to the Creator Himself, who is blessed forever and ever. Amen. [26-27] This is why God released them to their own vile pursuits, *and this is what happened*: they chose sexual

counterfeits—women had sexual relations with other women and men committed unnatural, shameful acts because they burned with lust for other men. This sin was rife, and they suffered painful consequences.

28 Since they had no mind to recognize God, He turned them loose to follow the unseemly designs of their depraved minds and to do things that should not be done. 29 Their days are filled with all sorts of godless living, wicked schemes, greed, hatred, endless desire for more, murder, violence, deceit, and spitefulness. And, *as if that were not enough,* they are gossiping, 30 slanderous, God-hating, rude, egotistical, smug people who are always coming up with even more dreadful ways to treat one another. They don't listen to their parents; 31 they lack understanding *and character.* They are simple-minded, covenant-breaking, heartless, and unmerciful; *they are not to be trusted.* 32 Despite the fact that they are fully aware that God's law says this way of life deserves death, they fail to stop. And *worse*—they applaud others on this destructive path.

I Corinthians 6:9-11

9-10 Do you need reminding that the unjust have no share in the blessings of the kingdom of God? Do not be misled. A lot of people stand to inherit nothing of God's coming kingdom, including those whose lives are defined by sexual immorality, idolatry, adultery, sexual deviancy, theft, greed, drunkenness, slander, and swindling. [11] Some of you used to live in these ways, but *you are different* now; you have been washed clean, set apart, restored, *and set on the right path* in the name of the Lord Jesus, the Anointed, by the Spirit of our living God.

1 Timothy 1:8-10

[8] You and I know the law is good (if used in the right way), and [9] we also know the law was not designed for law-abiding people but for lawbreakers and criminals, the ungodly and sin-filled, the unholy and worldly, the father killers and mother killers, the murderers, [10] the sexually immoral and homosexuals, slave dealers, liars, perjurers, and anyone else who acts against the sound doctrine [11] laid out in the glorious, *holy, and pure* good news of the blessed God that has been entrusted to me.

About the Author

At the age of almost 29, Daniel V. Runyon married the woman with whom he has shared an intimate life for 32 years, and in that relationship he discovered the joy and fulfillment designed by the Creator for the inhabitants of Eden.

Some issues addressed in this essay are treated at a deeper level in Runyon's novel *The Shattered Urn: An Allegorical History of the Universe* available on Amazon in both print and eBook format.

http://www.amazon.com/Shattered-Urn-Allegorical-History-Universe/dp/1878559168/ref=sr_1_7?s=books&ie=UTF8&qid=1423227855&sr=1-7

80578686R00048

Made in the USA
Columbia, SC
19 November 2017